A Life

BLESSED FRANCIS XAVIER SEELOS

Redemptorist

1819–1867

A Life of
BLESSED FRANCIS XAVIER SEELOS

Redemptorist

1819–1867

Carl W. Hoegerl, C.Ss.R.
and Alicia von Stamwitz

Liguori
LIGUORI, MISSOURI

Published by The Seelos Center
919 Josephine Street
New Orleans, LA 70130
www.seelos.org

Produced by Liguori Publications
Liguori, MO 63057
www.liguori.org

ISBN 978-0-7648-0651-3

Library of Congress Catalog Card Number: 00–100816

Printed in the United States of America
18 17 16 15 14 / 11 10 9 8 7

CONTENTS

FOREWORD

Reflecting on the life of Blessed Francis X. Seelos one is reminded of Søren Kierkegaard's definition of being a saint: *someone who can will the one thing.* Most people want to identify with the values of a dedicated person like Mother Teresa or Martin Luther King who gave her or his life to one thing: God and the poor or God and human rights. Even though we admire the lives of the saints, the problem is we want to be a saint and still experience the rest of life—seizing every opportunity to satisfy our needs for comfort, pleasure, and gratification. How do we live a simple lifestyle and, at the same time, long for the comforts of the rich and famous! We want to have solitude with God, but we don't want to miss every chance to party, go to movies, read, talk and be with friends. It is no surprise that for more and more people there is less and less time to experience and do everything. The result is a growing sense of being pulled in a thousand directions, fragmented, unfulfilled, and tired.

Although Blessed Francis Seelos lived and ministered in the nineteenth century, his story is still alive and fresh for us who are entering the twenty-first century. The life of Father Seelos teaches us that every choice is a limitation and every limitation is an opportunity for fulfillment beyond the self. To choose one thing is to accept the limitation of not doing many others. To choose to be a priest is not to be a movie idol or rock star. To be a religious with the vow of poverty is to let go of the economic prosperity of a business tycoon. To pray is to risk giving up one's self as one understands self. It is not easy to be a saint—*to will the one thing*—to live the single-minded commitment of Mother Teresa or Martin Luther King or Blessed Francis X. Seelos. The danger is that tasting all of life we are starved of the one thing that gives life.

The life of Blessed Francis Seelos can be understood within a single phrase: "The Spirit of God is upon me to bring Good News to the poor and to heal the brokenhearted" (Lk 4:18).

Because of his diligence, application, and self-sacrifice, Father Seelos is a model for all Christians. The burning desire to be a missionary in America demanded that he study foreign languages; that he practice self-discipline in preparation for hardships he would encounter on the mission; that he leave his homeland forever; that he venture as a poor immigrant to a land of penniless immigrants; that he risk his life to bring redemptive presence to the poor, the disenfranchised, and the terminally ill qualifies him eminently as a person who *willed the one thing.*

In every aspect of life, Father Seelos shows us how to relate to God and one another—how to pray, how to search for healing, how to seek forgiveness and reconciliation, how to ask for guidance, how to understand community, religious experience, and vocation.

I hope this biography of Blessed Francis X. Seelos will inspire you to integrate into your own life the human and the divine and to be committed to *willing the one thing*: that the Spirit of Jesus become enfleshed in your life.

Thomas D. Picton, C.Ss.R.
Vice-Provincial Superior
Redemptorists
New Orleans Vice-Province

INTRODUCTION

Opening a biography of Blessed Francis Xavier
Seelos (1819–1867) is like opening a window
and taking in a great breath of fresh air. Here is an
irresistible modern spirituality, made visible and particular by an otherwise ordinary immigrant priest.
Brimming with youthful courage and idealism, Francis left his German homeland at age twenty-four to
join a handful of Redemptorist missionaries in the
New World. What he found in the United States was
hardly romantic: the swelling immigrant population
was stumbling under the weight of poverty, sickness,
loneliness, and rejection. But Francis did not quit or
give up.

Day after day, he brought the tender and trans-
forming love of Jesus Christ to people without hope.
His friendly, loving nature radiated joy as he worked

to lighten the burden of so many sorrowful lives. Unlike most great saints, he was not a powerful prelate, mystic, or martyr. He did not produce any significant writings or leave a lasting mark on the theological community. Rather, he left a lasting mark on the individual men, women, and children whom he helped through direct and personal attention to their daily needs. He is a model of simple, wholehearted service to God and neighbor, pointing the way to deep union with God through the familiar circumstances of contemporary human life.

Francis Seelos served the Roman Catholic Church in the United States of America during a critical period in its history. Before the 1820s, the fledgling Church had managed to provide adequate pastoral care for the steady but relatively slow stream of Catholic immigrants. But by the time Francis landed in New York in 1843, huge waves of new immigrants had stretched to breaking point the Church's resources and ministers. The Germans, in particular, were in dire straits because few priests spoke their language. Consequently, many either stopped practicing their faith or joined a non-

Catholic denomination. The Catholic bishops of the New World were painfully aware of the urgent pastoral needs of these new immigrants—much like the present-day situation of the Spanish-speaking community in the United States.

Beginning in the 1830s, the American bishops made frequent appeals to the European Church for help. Among the first to respond was Father Joseph Passerat, C.Ss.R., superior of all Redemptorists north of the Alps. In 1832, six members of the Congregation of the Most Holy Redeemer, three priests and three brothers, arrived in America.

Eleven years later, Francis joined the pioneer Redemptorist missionaries, devoting the rest of his life to pastoral service in the U.S. Church as parish priest, mission preacher, seminary professor and director of students, catechist, and confessor. He was exceptionally gifted in some areas, most notably as an effective confessor and lively preacher, but his holiness proceeds primarily from his faithfulness to his daily duties. "Be faithful in little things," Francis advised a student. "Pray fervently and all will go well" (Curley, Michael J., *Cheerful Ascetic: The Life of Francis Xavier Seelos, C.Ss.R.*, New Orleans Vice Province, 1969, p. 140).

Twenty-four years after his arrival in New York, Father Seelos died of yellow fever. By this time he was beloved by immigrants and established citizens alike. Thousands of mourners of different races, nationalities, and classes crowded together in St. Mary's Assumption Church in New Orleans, waiting hours for a chance to pray before his casket. The children and grandchildren of these mourners guarded his memory, seeking his intercession and promoting his cause for canonization. On April 9, 2000, in a ceremony at the Vatican, Pope John Paul II beatified Francis Xavier Seelos, recognizing his sanctity and preparing the way for his eventual canonization. Redemptorist Father Thomas D. Picton, vice-provincial superior of the Redemptorists' New Orleans Vice-Province, hailed the Vatican's decision. Father Seelos's beatification, said Father Picton, "is a testament to his life's work of mercy and compassion to welcome all people who experience themselves as strangers, alienated, marginalized, and disenfranchised into a new communion of the human family."

The lesson that springs from the life of Francis Xavier Seelos is a lesson taught by his spiritual father, Saint Alphonsus Liguori: "It is a great mistake to say, 'God doesn't want everyone to be a saint.' On the contrary...God wants all of us to be saints, and each one according to his or her state of life: the religious as a religious, laypeople as laypeople, the priest as a priest, the married person as married, the merchant as merchant, the soldier as a soldier, and so on, in every other state of life" (Alphonsus Liguori, *Practice of the Love of Jesus Christ*, Liguori Publications: Liguori, MO, 1997, p. 76).

Through his vocation to the priesthood and to religious life, Francis Xavier Seelos found the ultimate twin treasures: happiness and holiness.

BIOGRAPHICAL CHRONOLOGY OF BLESSED FRANCIS X. SEELOS, C.SS.R.

1819: January 11, Füssen, Germany: birth and baptism of Francis Xavier Seelos

1825–1831:
Elementary schooling

1828: September 3: Confirmation

1830: April 2: First Holy Communion

1831–1832:
Füssen: tutored by the hospital chaplain

1832–1839:
Augsburg: Saint Stephan's preparatory school and *Gymnasium*

1839–1841:
> Munich: Ludwig-Maximilian University, two years' study in philosophy

1841–1842:
> Munich: Ludwig-Maximilian University, one year study in theology

1842: Dillingen: Saint Jerome, diocesan seminary, until December 9

1843: Altötting: Saint Mary Magadalen, Redemptorist foundation

> March 17, Le Havre, France: sailed for the United States

> April 20, New York: arrived in the United States

> May 16, Baltimore: began his novitiate at Saint James's

1844: May 16, Baltimore: Saint James's: religious profession

> December 22, Baltimore: ordination to the priesthood

1845–1854:
> Pittsburgh, Pennsylvania: Saint Philomena parish, assistant priest

1851: Pastor and religious superior

1854–1857:
> Baltimore: Saint Alphonsus parish, pastor and religious superior

1857–1862:
> Cumberland, Maryland: Saints Peter and Paul parish, pastor, superior, prefect of students, and professor

May 1862–August 1865:
> Annapolis, Maryland: Saint Mary's parish, pastor and religious superior, prefect
>
> November 1862: Replaced as prefect of students at Annapolis
>
> May 1863–August 1865: Superior of the mission band

1865–1866:
> Detroit Michigan: Saint Mary's parish, assistant priest

1866–1867:

New Orleans, Louisiana: Saint Mary's Assumption parish, assistant priest and prefect of the German parish

1867: October 4, New Orleans, Louisiana: passed into eternal life

1

I HAVE CALLED YOU BY NAME

The story of Blessed Francis Xavier Seelos begins in Füssen, a picturesque town in the foothills of the German Alps. Situated on the ancient Roman road, the *Via Claudia*, Füssen has enjoyed a certain prominence from very early times. The

Picturesque Füssen

remains of Roman villas have been excavated nearby, and the summer residence of the prince-bishops of Augsburg, dating back to 1332, still dominates the area. In recent decades, this Bavarian town eighty miles southwest of Munich has become a favorite tourist site, especially for those who want to see the legendary castle *Neuschwannstein* built by King Ludwig II (1845–1886). The "enchanted castle," just a few miles outside of Füssen, has been immortalized by Walt Disney as a symbol of Disneyland.

In the early 1800s, the majority of the town's sixteen hundred residents were Catholic. Pictures of Jesus, the Blessed Virgin, and the saints adorned street corners and exterior walls. The surrounding countryside was dotted with wayside shrines and crucifixes, winning this region of Germany the name *Pfaffenwinkel*, or Priests' Corner.

Three churches held services in the town. The *Spitalkirche* (Hospital Church), the Franciscan *Frauenkirche*, and the parish church of Saint Mang, or Mangus. According to tradition, around A.D. 750, Saint Mang journeyed from Switzerland to the region to convert the pagans. He laid the foundation

Saint Mang's church, exterior

of a Benedictine community of monks that was to flourish more than a thousand years. The spiritual life of the community of Füssen revolved around the monastery of Saint Mang.

The parents of Francis Xavier, Mang Seelos and Frances Schwarzenbach, were married in the parish church of Saint Mang on October 28, 1811. "When our dear parents married," their daughter Antonia later wrote, "Füssen was still a town in the good old German tradition. Anyone who wanted to get married had to have a house and a piece of land for at least two cows, so that whenever the trade did not provide, there was something to live on."

The Seelos home was a three-story house of modest dimensions at what was then Number 184 *Spitalgasse* (Hospital Street). The ground floor served as a barn for domestic animals and a workplace for Mang's business. The house still stands today, with the address changed to Number 13 *Spitalgasse*. A bronze plaque, marking the birthplace of Blessed Francis Xavier Seelos, is affixed to it.

Mang was a weaver by trade in a community that also included farmers, merchants, masons, millers, and cloth-dyers. He was a skilled weaver, having mastered the art during a four-year apprenticeship in France. Unfortunately, the market began to weaken with the spread of the Industrial Revolution and his profits were never great. Only by combining his moderate earnings with hard work on the farm did

Spitalgasse where Seelos was born (house with name BIERIG on wall)

he and Frances manage to provide the essentials for their family.

Francis Xavier was the Seelos's sixth child, born in the family home on January 11, 1819, and baptized the same day in the parish church of Saint Mang. Frances would give birth to twelve children altogether: three died in infancy; three married; three entered the religious life; two chose the single life; one died at age nineteen after a tragic fall from a hayloft. An abandoned child whom Mang unexpectedly carried home one day would complete the Seelos family, a boy the family dubbed "Prince John" because he was the youngest and adored by all.

Mang Seelos was a devout German Catholic with a Frenchman's spirit, thanks to his extended sojourn in France. Anton Schirsner, a school friend of Francis's who lived with the Seelos family for five months in 1845, later described the colorful personality of Mang Seelos:

> How vividly that man stands before me! A well-rounded man, a self-made man, a perfect Catholic, the pattern of the father of a family, a man of penetrating intelligence and of firm and genuine

religious principles....His *elán,* his *verve,* [and] his *esprit* were unalloyed French characteristics of spirit....All during the day he often prattled away in French. Very often at his weaving he sang his French songs. He was always happy and in high spirits. He had, too, a warmth of disposition, as again only a Frenchman has, like a Francis de Sales. Once he began to sing with the blackbird he had hanging in front of the loom and I heard him sing to himself so soulfully: "Oh, you lovely little bird, sing right well the praises of your Creator."

Francis would inherit his father's joyful spirit as well as his quiet dignity. Anton continues:

This man had much to contend with, not only with the dumb crowd of his fellow townspeople, who did not understand and did not know him, but also with his own pastor, who from egoism and passion almost robbed the good man of his bread, and who, in the end, that is, on his death-bed, had to ask Mang for forgiveness. And still more: for a long time he had to fight "the fight for survival," so to speak, in the manner of Darwin. Such a large family, all with such good appetites, and for their entire subsistence only the proceeds of his weaving....[T]his could sometimes make one anxious.

Sacristan's house, Füssen

The Seelos's situation improved considerably in 1830 when Mang Seelos was offered the job of parish sacristan of Saint Mang's. From this point on, he was guaranteed a steady salary to supplement his income, and the family moved to a spacious house provided by the parish with a lovely garden on the property.

Frances Schwarzenbach Seelos was by all accounts a good match for Mang. She, too, cultivated a rich spiritual life, found pleasure in daily work, and had a sense of humor. Making light of the family's financial worries even as babies tumbled out one after another, she playfully called the children "my little debts."

Antonia, Francis's younger sister, described her mother as a woman very much in love with her husband and with God. "She prayed during all her work. She even knelt down in the field when she heard the bell for the consecration in some nearby church, or the Angelus. We children did not always like this frequent praying, but only as one gets older does one realize how important it is."

Years later, Francis would tell his Redemptorist

students that his uneducated mother was guided by the Holy Spirit in the education of her children. Even at the level of university studies, he said, the academic lectures he attended seemed merely a more scientific presentation of what he had already learned from his mother. For her part, Frances would later say, "He who stands, let him take care not to fall. I have not done more than what every Christian mother is supposed to do, only it struck deeper roots in my dear Xavier than in others."

A letter written by Antonia in 1883 provides a charming glimpse of the Seelos family's daily routine:

"Morning hours are golden hours" was [my father's] saying. All of us had to get up early. After everyone had been to Mass, each went to his work, and the little ones to school. At 12 noon, the Angelus was said by the whole family, and then the meal prayers. During the meal, father asked what we had learned in school, and always gave us good advice and encouragement. At table there were often ten of us, and during the summer often twelve. Almost every time, our brother Xavier brought along a student. After meals we said the table prayers. We girls then had to help mother in her work: in the summer in the garden and field; in winter, with sewing and knitting. We could not be idle for even a quarter of an hour. Our dear mother could herself teach us all kinds of work, and she was always the first at hard tasks as well as easy tasks, and always guided us in it with a word of encouragement. Our deceased father was very strict; everything had to be done right away and promptly. Still, at the same time, he was considerate if we admitted our mistake immediately and never told a lie. He did not punish much, but his scolding glance was more than a punishment for us....Our dear mother immediately always became our intercessor, and her request he never rejected.

A day in the Seelos home always ended with family prayer and spiritual reading, usually a passage on the life of the saint of the day. Once, when Francis was a child, his mother read aloud the story of his namesake, Saint Francis Xavier, the great Jesuit missionary to the East. Francis cried out excitedly: "I want to be a Francis Xavier!" Although this may sound like a thin piece of pious legend, in his teenage years Francis did, in fact, consider a vocation to the Jesuits. And, anyway, he ended up joining the Redemptorists, so a hagiographer keen on fabricating a perfect script should have had Francis cry out, "I want to be an Alphonsus Liguori!"

2

SCHOOL DAYS

Francis was a good-natured child who benefited from the love and attention of a close-knit family. His only serious difficulty was recurring illness. "It was believed that he would die as a child," his sister Antonia later wrote. "He often had severe intestinal pains and suffered from worms." His siblings entertained him when he was sick, sitting at his bedside and reading aloud to him. With such a large family, he was at least not too lonely during these long months of illness.

From age six to age twelve, Francis attended Füssen's primary school in a building that still stands on the corner of *Schrannengasse* and *Brunnengasse*. The century-old building was known as the *Kornhaus* because its main floor was used as a marketplace for grain. A large open room on the second

The *Kornhaus* now the *Feuerhaus*, the boyhood school

floor held up to sixty boys; girls attended classes in a separate building.

Due to a bout of illness, Francis began school late, in January of 1825. The fall semester typically began in November and ended around Easter. The summer semester began the first week of May and ended in August. Daily lessons were in two sessions: from 8:00 A.M. to 10:00 A.M. and from 1:00 P.M. to 3:00 P.M., six days a week, with Wednesday and Saturday afternoons free.

Although the school was run by the state, not by a Catholic parish, a priest was on the school board and each school day began with Mass at 7:30 A.M. The curriculum included the basic subjects—reading, writing, and arithmetic—as well as religious instruction and music. Francis learned to play the violin as a boy and, like his father, he loved to sing.

At the conclusion of his final year in primary school, Francis's schoolmaster noted that he had a "very great" innate ability. Of eleven areas, he earned the grade "excellent" in five: diligence, conduct, religion, reading, and handwriting. In the other six areas—spelling, composition, arithmetic, national history, practical crafts, and memory—he received the grade "very good."

During these childhood years in Füssen, Francis showed signs of a natural inclination toward prayer and religious devotion. Besides joining in the times of family prayer, he liked to pray the rosary before falling asleep at night. After his confirmation at age nine, he decided to become an altar server. Soon he had set up a small altar at home, decorated with care, where he held "services" with his friends. He was exceptionally kind to his friends, especially children poorer than himself, gladly sharing his clothes, a bit of food, or the small change in his pocket. In 1830, some eighteen months after his confirmation, he made his First Communion.

This spiritual bent did not prevent him from engaging in ordinary activities and childish pranks. When his health permitted, Francis enjoyed wandering outdoors and exploring the countryside. His appreciation of nature grew as he matured, and it remained strong throughout his life. As for innocent mischief, Francis once related a telling anecdote, which a student remembered and later recorded:

On one of the days of carnival...it occurred to our Xavier to dress up like the traditional clown. Secretly he dressed himself in his father's long-tailed wedding coat, put on his father's hat, and paraded up and down the street to the great delight of the entire neighborhood. His father, hearing the commotion, came out of the house and was not a little surprised to see his very special coat walking about.

Francis apparently enjoyed hamming it up and being the center of attention, but his father's reprimand was sharp enough to leave a lasting memory.

After graduation from primary school, Francis's future became problematical. A talented boy would ordinarily proceed to secondary studies at a four-year preparatory school which was followed by four years at a *Gymnasium* (a pre-university school specializing in classical subjects) in preparation for a professional career. Francis had the talent, the desire, and his parents' support to continue his studies, but the Seelos family could not afford tuition and board at a distant school.

Fortunately, Father Francis Anton Heim, pastor at Saint Mang, provided a solution. "I will help you," he said. "I am well known everywhere in Augsburg. I will see about your meal days and a monthly allowance. That way you will make it." After a one-year private tutorial in Füssen while arrangements were finalized, Francis entered the second year of preparatory classes at the Institute of Saint Stephan, Augsburg, ninety miles from his home. He would never again live at home for an extended period of time.

This was Francis's first experience of living in a large city, one of about thirty thousand residents, and among a large non-Catholic population. Augsburg was well known, of course, for its association with the Protestant Reformation. When Francis arrived at Saint Stephan's in October 1832, secular priests and laity staffed the school of more than six hundred students. In 1834, a notable change took place: King Ludwig I of Bavaria, "taking into consideration the petition of the Catholic citizens of Augsburg," established a Benedictine abbey at Saint Stephan's and entrusted to the Order the entire institute attached to it. The institute included the preparatory school, a *Gymnasium*, a seminary, a two-year lyceum, and a hospice for boys of nobility.

The courses offered at Saint Stephan's were in the long tradition of a classic, humanistic education, with a heavy concentration on Latin and Greek. During his seven years of study in Augsburg—three years in the preparatory school and four years in the *Gymnasium*—Francis was consistently in the top fifth of his class. His classes included religion, German, arithmetic and mathematics, geography and history. Besides these core subjects, there were elective classes in foreign languages, drawing, and music.

Francis received an honorable mention for his proficiency in French—which surely tickled *pere* Mang—and achieved the highest grade in his last year of the *Gymnasium*. Thanks again to Mang's incomparable example, one school friend remembers that Francis had an abnormally loud singing voice. "Seelos, don't shout so loud," the friend whispered one day, but Francis ignored him. "He didn't pay any attention to me; he was completely carried away by the enthusiasm of his soul. Once with several others we went into a church near his hometown. *Sans gene* he began to sing a hymn to Mary with the full power of his lungs, and he sang it all alone to the end, without paying any attention to the others."

The spiritual life of the students was of special concern at Saint Stephan's, both under the secular clergy and later the Benedictines. All the students attended daily Mass in the former convent church at 7:30 A.M. On Sundays and feast days, the priests celebrated High Mass and preached an additional sermon before or after Mass. In the afternoon, the students sang solemn vespers or attended a special devotional service. Four times a year, the students went to confession and Communion.

Francis did not live at the school, but lodged with a family that rented rooms to students, possibly in company with two cousins who were also at Saint Stephan's at the time. His circumstances were less than ideal: each day, he had to go to a different home at midday for his main meal. In the morning and in the evening he fended for himself, usually munching on a piece of dry bread.

His parents scraped together a weekly allowance of one florin—about fifty cents—which Francis often shared with other poor students, earning him the nickname, "Banker Seelos." When his parents found out about it and complained, Francis responded, "They are poorer than I am and do not have any meal days or money. I cannot stand seeing them going without as long as I have something."

He invited some of these needy students to spend summer vacations with his family. His favorite recreation, alone or with companions, was hiking in the nearby forest, soaking up the natural beauty of Füssen's rolling hills, clear lakes, and snowcapped mountains. He also liked to take long "walking trips," usually with a shrine as the destination.

When Francis was sixteen years old, he walked fifty hours to the shrine at the abbey church of Einsiedeln in Switzerland and asked to be admitted to the Benedictine monastery. The monks refused him, probably because of his youth. "He came home very sad," his sister Antonia later wrote. "Still in all this, he was not long-faced; he was always happy and cheerful. He also took part in entertainment, and during vacation he was always my dancing partner, because I was only a year younger than Xavier and we were the closest to each other. We shared together all our walks and diversions, and we unburdened to each other all our heartaches."

He also liked to take long walks with his father, and it was during one of their excursions together that a more mature Francis confided to Mang, and to no one else in the family, that he wished to follow the example of his namesake by becoming a missionary priest in a foreign land.

3

DISCERNING THE CALL

A few months after graduating from the *Gymnasium*, Francis chose to continue his studies at the University of Munich. The University had an excellent reputation, but it is somewhat surprising that Francis did not continue with the two-year

Munich University in 1840

course of philosophy offered by the Benedictines at Saint Stephan's lyceum.

Despite the fact that he was attracted to religious life, it seems that Francis needed more time to settle his mind. He hadn't yet ruled out the diocesan priesthood, which would enable him to remain in his homeland and close to his family. By studying philosophy at the University, he would be acquiring an academic formation that was indispensable for the priesthood. At the same time, he would still be able to enter the University of Munich's School of Theology if, at the end of the two years required for philosophy, he remained uncertain about his religious vocation.

Then, too, Francis was in the prime of his life and affectionate by nature, so of course he was attracted to women. As the moment of decision neared, the interior struggle between celibacy and marriage intensified, surfacing in his dreams. In one dream, which he later wrote down, he saw himself as a priest at the altar with the consecrated Host in his hand. He was about to give Communion to the faithful, but his eyes were distracted and fell upon an "unusually attractive" young woman. Quickly, he "recommended her to God and strove only to know and to fulfill the will of his divine Master." Also in this dream an image of the "sunny south, the land of oranges, swam before [his] eyes," which might be interpreted as a symbol of the appealing warmth of marital intimacy.

In Munich, Francis lived with two Füssen cousins in rented rooms at Number 20 *Karlsplatz,* a short distance from the University. His tuition was paid by a stipend for poor students that the town council

20 Karlsplatz (left) Seelos's boardinghouse, Munich

of Füssen had awarded him the previous month. He tutored in his free time in order to help cover incidental expenses. On Sundays, he taught his brother Adam, who was also in Munich for the purpose of learning a trade, how to write.

A typical university student, Francis learned to fence, to dance, and to snuff tobacco. He liked to write poetry, especially when he was sad or sick. Though not in the highest grade level for the four semesters of philosophy, he was in the second highest percentile of the class and easily qualified for continuing studies.

In 1841, he began his studies in theology. He elected to take traditional courses—systematic theology, moral theology, Church history, scriptural exegesis, pedagogy, and Hebrew—and received grades noticeably higher than he had in philosophy. If Francis had decided at this point to become a diocesan priest, he would have moved into special quarters to live with other seminarians. Again, he hesitated. He was waiting, it seems, for a sign from God or an interior certainty about his future.

Sometime during his first or second semester of

theology studies, Francis received the confirmation he was waiting for. His brother Adam later reported, "One Sunday, when I came to him for my writing lesson, he said to me: 'Today we will not write. Last night the Blessed Mother appeared to me. I have to become a missionary.' Whether she appeared to him visibly or only in a dream, I cannot say. I did not inquire further, because I felt very sad that I was to lose my dear brother."

This Marian vision or dream, coupled with a compelling Redemptorist appeal for missionaries to the New World, convinced Francis Xavier Seelos of his vocation to the Congregation of the Most Holy Redeemer. Sometime in the spring of 1842, he left the University, interrupting his theology studies, and sent a letter of application to the superior of the Redemptorists in the United States. The response did not come immediately; on November 3, anxiously biding his time, Francis entered the Augsburg diocesan seminary. The acceptance letter arrived three weeks later.

Francis was ecstatic. The next morning, he made arrangements to withdraw from the seminary. A rapturous notice in the *Augsburger Postzeitung* marked Francis's departure:

> Dillingen, December 9. This morning, there departed from the diocesan seminary here one of its most worthy members, Francis Xavier Seelos (born in Füssen, 1819), to leave for North America and there, after entering the Redemptorist Order in Baltimore, to dedicate himself for his entire life to the important vocation of a missionary. May the Lord accompany with superabundant blessing this truly apostolic undertaking of so worthy a follower of the great apostle of India, Francis Xavier, and at the same time, may this example of rare courage and apostolic zeal also inspire many other priests and seminarians of the clergy in Catholic Bavaria, endowed with the same necessary qualities of heart and spirit, to follow in his footsteps, for the words of the Savior still apply to the northern half of America in a special way, "The harvest is indeed great but the laborers are few. Ask therefore the master of the harvest to send laborers into his vineyard."

Francis's announcement that he was joining the Redemptorist missionaries in the New World stunned almost everyone. His family members had known for a long time that he was considering the priesthood, but they had always presumed that he would enter a local religious community or the diocesan priesthood and remain close to home. When he entered the Augsburg diocesan seminary, they were delighted and began chatting among themselves about attending his First Mass.

Only Mang knew about the letter of application to the Redemptorists in America. As Francis kissed each family member good-bye on the last day of what would be their final vacation together, Mang caught his son's eye and pointed to the sky. Francis caught the meaning of the wordless gesture: they would see each other again in heaven.

Four months would pass between the arrival of Francis's acceptance letter and his departure for America, but he deliberately chose not to visit his family again because he believed it would be too painful for them all. In this, too, he followed the example of Saint Francis Xavier, who left for the missions in India without seeing his family a final time.

The flurry of letters Francis sent home during these final months in Europe reveal the depth of his affection for his family and the breadth of his faith. To his cousin Benedict he wrote,

> If I had to depend only on my own strength, I would lose all confidence and courage in such an undertaking. But when I think of the help of God, when I consider his promises, when I take into account his power and his goodness, everything within me comes alive again, and I feel strong and powerful enough to work in the vineyard of the Lord. Even if far away from home, I am close to him who has called me to this work.

To his brother Adam, Francis wrote, "If it were up to me alone, I would always stay with you and our family, but I will not and cannot resist the inner call that comes from the other side, but I will give myself freely with entire love."

Finally, to his younger sister Antonia with whom he shared an especially strong bond, he wrote,

Even though I am far away, love remains and unites us eternally, here in prayer for one another, there in a joyful meeting without parting. When your duties become burdensome, when your heart is heavy, think of your dear brother. He is praying for you. When my duties become burdensome, when my heart is heavy, I will quickly think of you and say to myself, "See, your loving sister is praying for you." I am writing this not without tears, and you will be crying too.... Farewell forever, dearest, unforgettable sister!

4

MISSIONARY
TO THE NEW WORLD

Before he could sail to America, Francis had to collect all of his important papers and apply for the necessary travel documents. On December 27, 1842, he obtained a passport, which gives a detailed description of his physical traits.

Age:	24 years old
Height:	6 feet
Hair:	brown
Forehead:	rounded
Eyebrows:	brown
Eyes:	brown
Nose:	thick
Mouth:	large
Beard:	brown

Chin:	round
Face:	oval
Complexion:	healthy
Other marks:	none

During these months of preparation, Francis stayed in a Redemptorist community for the first time. Although he was with the Altötting community only briefly, one story is worth recounting. On the night of Francis's arrival at the Redemptorist monastery, he noticed that his shoes were dirty from traveling. He was a neat person, so he carefully placed his shoes outside his room in order that the brother porter might clean and polish them. The next morning he found the shoes just where he had left them, and just as dirty. It was Francis's first lesson in an unwritten Redemptorist rule: If you want something done, go right ahead and do it!

Once his papers were in order, Francis proceeded to France. He had eight days to sightsee in Paris and thought constantly and happily of his father. On March 17, 1843, he and three other Redemptorists met at the port of Le Havre and set sail on the

American packet ship *Saint Nicholas*, "a new and beautiful ship," he noted with boyish excitement.

Despite fearful storms at sea and sickness on board, Francis remained cheerful through most of the five-week journey. He made friends among his one hundred fifty fellow passengers, taught some of them catechism, and shared the wine he had brought with him. Only toward the end of the voyage did he become homesick and depressed, partly because he

The *Saint Nicolas*

had hoped to arrive in New York in time to celebrate Holy Week.

On Good Friday, he soothed himself in customary fashion by writing a poem. The rhyme and meter are lost in this literal translation of a selection from the German manuscript, but the sentiment is clear.

> O sacred splendor of the quiet night,
> when Christ, in his grave,
> found respite from his sufferings
> and relief from his bodily pains.
>
> All through this same night,
> My Father keeps vigil,
> folding his hands to Jesus,
> gazing at him in the Sacrament.
>
> Joining in prayer with her husband,
> My dear Mother also keeps vigil,
> Praying and shedding her tears of sorrow,
> During this night of watchful expectation.

During the same solemn night,
On the sea their son is far from home
For him the stars shine as sacristy lamps
As he also keeps vigil…

The sea is empty and barren—
only dangers and perils abound,
Nowhere is a church to be seen,
Nowhere an altar for the Sacrament.

On this night of sorrow,
my glance turns back to home;
uniting my heart with my parents' prayers
for the son they sorely miss and
    the Savior they await.

On Thursday, April 20, the *Saint Nicolas* finally docked in New York's spacious harbor. Father Gabriel Rumpler, superior of the New York foundation on Second Street, welcomed the travelers. He was one of fifteen Redemptorist missionaries already in the United States at the time: ten priests and five brothers. The Redemptorists had been ministering in the eastern states, primarily among poor immigrants, for just over a decade.

Within a month of his arrival in New York, Francis was sent to the Redemptorist novitiate at Saint James parish in Baltimore. The new American novitiate lacked the standard supply of spiritual books and devotional items, but the residence was comfortable. Sometimes Francis had several companions in the novitiate, sometimes only one; and for a period he was alone. Overall, he was content.

Top: Sketch of St. James, Baltimore
Right: Alexander Czvitkovicz, C.Ss.R., pastor of St. James

"In peace and quiet I was able to make my novitiate while learning to practice the duties of a cleric," he wrote to his family. "I learned to love the spiritual life and its treasures more and more. God planted deep in my heart the desire to offer myself completely to Him. This desire grows from day to day, so that I want to give God more than I have ever done before, all I ever held dear, all to which my heart was once attached."

On May 16, 1844, after a full year in the novitiate, Francis took his vows as a Redemptorist. On December 22, 1844, he was ordained to the priesthood in Saint James church, Baltimore. He wrote to his family,

> On Christmas Day, between six and eight o'clock in the morning, I first celebrated two private Masses, and at ten o'clock I could celebrate High Mass....I certainly did include all of you in them and recommended you to him whom I held so closely before me and touched with my own hands, and [whom I] offered and took into my heart. If only you had experienced it. Holy Guardian Angels, tell it to them, so that they can share in the joy, share in my prayers.

This is part of a charming, lengthy letter Francis wrote to his family in August 1845, which also describes in colorful detail other events and experiences of his first two years in America. He struggles with "the bedbugs, the insects, the religious sects, the language, and so many things more...the vulgar spirit of speculation, business, and money, the coldness and dryness of the people—nowhere a cross or a church of pilgrimage—no happy faces, no songs, no singing, everything dead."

"Nonetheless," he continues in the next paragraph, "I love my way of life....I am always as healthy as can be and do not want for the smallest thing—the best food, decent clothing. We have heat and water in the house, which can be used all through the night."

Addressing his father, Francis devotes a lighthearted paragraph to the subject of snuff, which he found "very good" in America but which his novice master suggested he give up. "For a long time, I snuffed with great relish, but the reverend novice master advised me to try to give up snuffing completely. No sooner said than done, and now, for over a year, I have not taken a single pinch, and with the grace of God, I will not take one again, until, dear father, I find you again in heaven, where I am sure you will immediately offer me a good pinch of genuine Bolongaro. That the saints in heaven also have snuff, one of our fathers, who is not adverse to it, has clearly verified, because even an angel once brought tobacco to a pious snuffer, who out of love for God had come to be in great need of it and had been hankering for it for a long time with the utmost self-denial. Therefore, be of good cheer, dear father, until once again we go snuffing together."

Finally, he writes in a somber tone of the difficulties ahead and dedicates himself anew. "If I had acted according to my own will and choice, I would never have set my foot on American soil... [but] with both arms, and with all my imagination and enthusiasm, I have embraced this dullness and ordinariness of America. The poverty and neglect of the greatest portion of the Germans, instruction of their children, and with time, even more, that of the Blacks, since they are here, provide superabundant material to lay claim to all the activity of a priest who wants to dedicate himself fully to the well-being of his neighbor."

The dream Francis had harbored in secret for so many years had become reality, and Francis, as we will see, was ready to "fight the good fight of the faith" (1 Tim 6:12).

5

PARISH PRIEST:
THE FIRST DECADE

Shortly after his ordination Father Seelos, as we will now call him, plunged into parish work. He remained in Baltimore for eight months assisting at Saint James parish. In the fall of 1845, he was assigned to Saint Philomena's in Pittsburgh, Pennsylvania, where he would spend the next nine years. Saint Philomena's was called the "Factory Church" because the makeshift church building originally was a factory. The decrepit structure was too small to accommodate even one-third of the parishioners who crowded inside for services; later, though, the Redemptorists would build a new church, which was dedicated on the first Sunday of October 1846.

Near the former factory building, another leaky, cramped building served as the rectory. This building

Old St. Philomena's church, Pittsburgh

was Father Seelos's first residence in Pittsburgh, and it was too small even for the three priests assigned

there: Redemptorists John Neumann, Joseph Mueller, and Francis Seelos, who were later to be joined by Father Hotz.

Saint John Neumann, Seelos's superior

Despite the primitive conditions, Father Seelos thrived under the guidance and care of the rector of the community, Father John Neumann—later named bishop—who was canonized in 1977, and is now known as Saint John Neumann. He later described his relationship with this exemplary Redemptorist.

> I was his subject but more like a son who needed help, for I had just left the novitiate and was inexperienced. In every respect he was a remarkable father to me. He introduced me to the practical life; he guided me as my spiritual leader and confessor. He cared for all my needs in body and soul; above all, the example of his virtues is vivid

in my memory, his tender modesty, his great humility, and his insuperable patience. Our dwelling was so poor that one night we had to leave our room in a severe storm and seek protection elsewhere, because the water was pouring down on our beds. I say our room because we were in one and the same room, which was separated only by a curtain. For that reason I could hear him often saying his prayers during the night. He slept so little that I could not understand how he could keep his body and soul together. Because he generally got up before the regular rising time, he prepared the fire, often bringing up coal himself to have the room warm for me when I got up (Curley, Michael J., *Cheerful Ascetic: The Life of Francis Xavier Seelos*, New Orleans Vice Province, 1969, p. 65).

With only twenty-one priests to care for forty-five thousand Catholics in western Pennsylvania, the bishop of Pittsburgh Michael O'Connor—along with the Redemptorists—faced a daunting pastoral situation. To reach isolated Catholic families on the outskirts of the diocese, the Redemptorists sometimes had to travel up to one hundred miles in miserable weather and over rough terrain.

In addition, these early years of ministry encompassed a time of bigotry and Catholic persecution in America. Hostile gangs routinely threatened and heckled Catholics in public; some threw torches at church buildings, setting them on fire. It took more than a little courage for the

Bishop Michael O'Connor

Redemptorists to venture out into the city streets or countryside to fulfill their pastoral duties.

Pittsburgh itself was a boisterous, expanding city of thirty thousand. Immigrants found plentiful if low-paying jobs in the city's factories, iron foundries, coal furnaces, and glassworks. Nonetheless, the more educated and well-off Pittsburghers scorned these newcomers as they strove to surmount dismal living conditions, illness, and economic insecurity.

Father Neumann catapulted Father Seelos into a fast-paced schedule that included celebrating marriages and baptisms, visiting the sick, hearing confessions, and preaching in three languages—

German, French, and English. Despite his broken, heavily accented English, people were captivated by Father Seelos's sermons. His message was simple, but his preaching style was unconventional and highly entertaining. Drawing on his storytelling talent, he would often act out Scripture narratives, ad-libbing extended conversations between Jesus, the disciples, and other gospel characters. Planting a fist first on one hip and then the other as he changed voices, he breathed life into gospel figures and injected humor and humanity into the familiar stories. Inevitably, "Jesus" would veer from his historical lines: he'd make pointed asides to the people, share wry observations on the gospel passage, and crack jokes. The people were delighted.

These sermons were by no means as spontaneous as they appeared. Father Seelos spent hours writing his text word for word. Midway through a sermon he would stop, wait for the people to quiet down, then continue in a more serious tone of voice. He would explain the Scriptures and drive home the practical implications for his listeners. His closing was like an evangelical minister's "altar call." He would extend his arms wide and cry out: "O you sinners who have not courage to confess your sins because they are so numerous or so grievous or so shameful! O, come without fear or trembling! I promise to receive you with all mildness; if I do not keep my word, I here publicly give you permission to cast it up to me in the confessional and to charge me with a falsehood!"

His preaching and promise to "receive all with mildness" spurred even timid or guilt-ridden Catholics to seek him out. At times, the line outside his confessional would snake through the church and out the door, creating a two- or three-hour wait for penitents. Father Seelos's gentle, friendly manner made it easy for penitents to confide in him, and his confidence in God's mercy lifted their spirits. "It is not your justice but God's mercy which is the motive of your trust," he preached. "He is the God of all consolations and the Father of mercies. He does not wish the death of a sinner but that he be converted and live. He came to heal the sick and to seek those who were lost. He spared the woman taken in adultery. He showed mercy to the thief crucified with him. He took upon himself our punishment.

He prayed for his murderers. He now intercedes for us at the right hand of God. No one was ever lost because his sin was too great, but because his trust was too small!"

Father Seelos had harsh words for priests who did not receive penitents with kindness and grace. "The priest who is rough with the people does injury to himself and to others," he said. "He sins, at least in ignorance…[and] he scandalizes all who see him and hear him….Thousands reject the Church and the sacraments and perish in eternity solely because they have been badly treated by a priest."

Nor did Father Seelos have any patience for religious who complained about the hardships of their vocation or who blamed their sufferings on others. To his two sisters in religious life he would later write,

> Would that all religious possessed sufficient faith, combined with courage and self-denial. This would enable them to see in their daily duties, in the commands of their superiors, in the various unforeseen occurrences of every day, in despondency and wretchedness of every kind,

the cross sent to them individually and especially by God. ...It is neither our confreres, nor our sisters in religion, nor even our superiors, who occasion these little sufferings. We deceive ourselves and give in to temptation if we consider ourselves ill-used by our community. The good God always stands in the background. He allows us to suffer how much and for as long as this is good for us.

In addition to Father Seelos's gift for preaching and competency in the confessional, he had a way with children. The Redemptorists set up a small schoolhouse near the "Factory Church" where Father Seelos taught catechism two or three times a week. He soon became a favorite visitor. "We children loved and revered him," a former student later wrote. "So great was the impression his holiness made on me that I used to walk after him imperceived, carefully placing my feet in the same marks made by his. I thus tried literally to walk in his footsteps."

Another student recalled that Father Seelos was quick to join the children in recreation and "merrymaking," playing in their sports and games and laughing heartily at their antics. In the schoolroom, however, he was more serious. "He was all kindness and gentleness. He explained religious truths very simply, but with so much feeling and earnestness that the most giddy in the little crowd would listen with attention."

Preparing the children for their First Communion, he impressed upon them the importance of the moment by listing all the kinds of martyrdom that he would willingly undergo rather than see any of them receive the Lord carelessly. "It was in speaking of the Most Blessed Sacrament that his ardent love shone forth," the student continues. "He used to say that the thought of the love and goodness of Jesus for us as shown in this Divine Sacrament almost deprived him of his senses. He was often so overcome by emotion during such discourses as to be obliged to pause for some moments."

His spirituality was not just a matter of pious words and sentiments. During his years in Pittsburgh, stories began to circulate of his generosity and kindness to the poor. There was nothing spectacular about his response to the needs around him; he did not have the skills or the call to start immense projects. Rather, he reached out in simple, practical ways such as giving his gloves to a freezing passerby, swapping boots with a man whose own boots were torn and useless, or washing a pile of laundry for a woman who was ill. One Redemptorist later recalled, "A poor woman who earned her living by taking in washing had a sick child, at whose bedside she had to watch during the night. Because of her hard work during the day and the lack of sleep at night, the woman was so exhausted that she could hardly move. Father Seelos came to her house at various times and kept watch over the child in place of the mother, so that she could get some rest."

For the most part, his help was received with gratitude, but he had a few unpleasant incidences during this time of strong anti-Catholic sentiment. Once, responding to a sick call, he was met at the door by a man who quickly locked all the doors behind him and without cause brutally beat Father Seelos. On other occasions, he was pelted by rocks, threatened at gunpoint, and nearly thrown overboard while on a ferry simply because he had knelt on the dock to show reverence to the consecrated Host he carried with him.

It was not an easy time to be a priest in America, but over the course of this first decade of Father Seelos's ministry, the picture that was gradually emerging was that of a passionate and fiercely committed priest. "As long as there is breath in me, with your help and grace, I will never give up," he wrote in his retreat notes from this period. "I am fully prepared for everything and give my body, and my soul completely into your hands as a holocaust....I want to die in the Catholic Church, in the holy Congregation."

6

MARYLAND
PARISH MINISTRY AND
DIRECTOR OF SEMINARY STUDENTS

In March of 1854, Father Seelos was transferred from Pittsburgh and appointed pastor of Saint Alphonsus parish in Baltimore. Eleven years of parish ministry followed at three different Maryland parishes: Saint Alphonsus's in Baltimore, Saints Peter and Paul parish in Cumberland, and Saint Mary's in Annapolis. During much of this time, he wore three hats as pastor of a parish, superior of a Redemptorist community, and director of students at the Redemptorist seminary.

Saint Alphonsus was the German-speaking national parish in Baltimore encompassing three other congregations and various other Catholic groups. In addition to Saint Alphonsus parish, the Redemp-

Saint Alphonsus's church, Baltimore

torists were responsible for two "outmissions," Saint James's and Saint Michael's, each about a mile away. Moreover, the Redemptorists were in the process of organizing a new German-Catholic center in the Federal Hill section of the city with the establishment of Holy Cross church. The black Catholics were also under their care, as well as a school for black children run by the Oblate Sisters of Providence. The administration of this parish was complex, and the pastoral needs were endless.

Once again, Father Seelos plunged into the bustling world of parish ministry, and once again he was careful to make time for the personal needs of the least among his congregation—even when it was most inconvenient. His confreres said that he routinely went to bed fully dressed or slept on a bench near the front door so that he could respond quickly to the inevitable late-night sick call. The prostitutes in one Baltimore house would never forget the night that Father Seelos hurried to comfort a young woman on her deathbed. He stayed with her till the end, knowing full well that his long, late-night visit would spark rumors. A few days later, when an anxious friend showed him a newspaper headline insinuating the obvious, he laughed and said simply, "Let the fellows talk on. I saved a soul."

In Maryland as in Pennsylvania, he was a much sought-after confessor. Some felt that he had "a power that others did not possess," namely, the ability to read hearts or to see deeply beyond the surface of their words. He also attracted and won many converts. Among them was a young widow whose husband had died while working on the exterior of the church. Father Seelos's kindness after her husband's death made such an impression that she decided to take instructions in the Catholic faith. The Reverend Cleveland Coxe, her minister and the future Episcopal Bishop of Western New York, got wind of the situation and intervened. He marched over to the rectory and insisted on debating with Father Seelos in the widow's presence. But the widow broke up the debate early, saying, "Mr. Coxe, it would be superfluous for you to continue further. Only now do I clearly see that the Roman Catholic Church is the true Church."

Routine matters, of course, occupied much of

Father Seelos's time. "From morning till night I am overwhelmed with cares and worries," he wrote to his sister during this period. "White and Black, German and English, confreres and externs, clerical and laypeople, aristocratic women and unworldly nuns, the poor, the sick, ask for my assistance. One wants this, the other that. There is no rest. It takes a real effort to snatch a little time for spiritual reading or a visit to the Blessed Sacrament. Could I write you an account of the experiences of even one day, you would be astonished."

Hearing the frustration in this letter, it is significant that most people saw him as easygoing and approachable. One community member later said, "Although he was superior and his attention was much in demand, it was never too much for him to converse about a half-hour with the poor idiot who received his dinner at the monastery. He patiently encouraged the poor man, trying to place himself in his circumstances in order to understand him better."

Another confrere was not so understanding. He berated Father Seelos one day for "scandalously wasting time" with a poor, eccentric elderly woman that he had spent hours consoling. Father Seelos answered, "I do nothing wrong in receiving all kindly, without distinction. It would be wrong to receive some affably and some rudely."

The dizzying pace of Father Seelos's pastoral life eventually had an effect on his health. In March of 1857, he felt cold and stiff one day after hearing confessions. He was exercising in place to get his circulation going when blood suddenly spurted from his mouth. Father Seelos wasn't alarmed and went about his work the rest of the afternoon, but his fellow Redemptorists informed the provincial. The provincial ordered Father Seelos to bed. The doctor who examined him determined that he had broken a blood vessel in his throat and that he would have to remain quiet in bed for an extended period of time if he were to survive.

Father Seelos's throat did begin to heal, but the provincial decided that a change was in order and reassigned him to the relative quiet of formation work. "I regard this change as absolutely necessary," the provincial wrote, "if Father Seelos is not to be exposed to the danger of a relapse within a short time, and to the risk of being forever rendered unfit for work. If I leave him working here in Baltimore I might not be able to control him, and in a short time, he will certainly ruin himself."

Father Seelos was appointed pastor of Saints Peter and Paul Church, a small church in Cumberland, Maryland, and "prefect," or director, of Redemptorist students in the attached seminary. As prefect he was in charge of the spiritual formation and general welfare of about sixty students from at least six different nations, and he would also teach

Saints Peter and Paul Seminary

at the seminary. The first year, he was ordered to take it easy and to refrain from preaching publicly and singing High Masses to allow his throat to heal fully. In August he wrote, "My health has been so restored that I am able to perform all my duties and still find time for prayer and study. I continue to feel the wounded spot up to now but it gives me no pain or annoyance."

Father Seelos was a natural in his new role as father figure, mentor, model, and friend to the Redemptorist students. He was a genuinely happy religious, so it was easy for him to communicate the love and respect he had for the Congregation and its members. As for his new role of professor, he prepared carefully for his lectures and, for the most part, enjoyed giving them. He wrote to a religious friend, in passable English,

> I have to teach theology, dogmatic and exegesis…. To enable the Fathers of our Congregation to be well prepared for the confessional, our chief study is moral theology; but I could never find a particular taste in that study, and it was only an act of virtue when I forced myself to that study,

for more than a 100 reasons; but the doctrinal, historical and exegetical part of the theologie [sic] ever was and ever will be my greatest delight; for truly it leads to our after world, near to God (Curley, Michael J., *Cheerful Ascetic: The Life of Francis Xavier Seelos, C.Ss.R.*, Vice Province of New Orleans, 1969, p. 165).

While the students did not have an abundance of food or comfort, they did have a great affection for Father Seelos. Outside of the classroom, he was approachable and playful; he loved to join the students in their recreation. They would often go on long "walking trips" with Father Seelos at the head, singing and telling stories and generally having more fun than all of them put together. When the students complained that he always sang the same hymn, he replied with a smile, "Once beautiful, always beautiful."

Three of the students formed what they called the "Laughing Society." Father Seelos was curious about it and asked if he could join. After a brief consultation he was admitted. The rules of the society were: At any time a member could be called on to crack a joke. But no one was permitted to laugh until a signal was given. First a consultation was to take place, to decide whether the joke deserved a laugh or a grunt. If a laugh, all members had to start laughing and then immediately stop at the signal. The one who laughed last got a penance of prayers. Father Seelos could easily start laughing, but unfortunately he could never stop once he got going. After "winning" several hefty penances, he sheepishly asked permission to resign.

In April 1861, the bloody American Civil war began, shattering the peace and quiet of the Cumberland seminary. Since Maryland was a border state, the threat of a battle in the area was real. In June, a rumor that the Redemptorist seminary was hiding guns and ammunition prompted a forced search. A more serious incident took place in August when seminarians playing a game near the Virginia border were mistaken for an attacking army. In short, seminary life in Cumberland was growing more uncomfortable with each passing month.

In the spring of 1862, Father Seelos and his students moved to the Redemptorist foundation in

Annapolis, Maryland. The property on which this foundation stood was formerly the estate of Charles Carrol of Carrolton, the only Catholic signer of the Declaration of Independence. Father Seelos was appointed religious superior of the community and pastor of Saint Mary's church, to which the new seminary was attached. He loved the new, spacious seminary property with terraced gardens and a beautiful view of Chesapeake Bay in the distance. That

St. Mary's Seminary and Church

summer, he scheduled time each day for the students to visit the Redemptorists' waterfront property and take a dip. "Salt water," he said, "refreshes the body and strengthens the limbs."

On March 3, 1863, President Abraham Lincoln signed the Conscription Act, which stipulated that all men twenty to forty-five years of age could be drafted unless they could pay three hundred dollars (equivalent to about two years' pay for a Union Private) for a substitute. The Redemptorists could not afford to pay the exemption fee, of course, and grew concerned that their youngest charges might be suddenly forced to enter the army.

After the Battle of Gettysburg (July 1–3, 1863), Father Seelos's anxieties increased. "Next Monday," he announced to his confreres, "I go to Washington City to see, if possible, Father Abraham and have a talk with him about the draft. If I do not succeed in obtaining a release from that unjust injunction, we will rather go to prison than to take up arms." Together with another confrere, Father Seelos did in fact see the President. President Lincoln received them kindly but was unable to assure them that the students would be exempt from draft calls. As it happened, none of the students had to enter military service.

Despite Father Seelos's efforts to serve his religious community well and faithfully, some of his confreres had difficulty with his methods. Others were perhaps jealous of his popularity. In either case, around this time a few influential Redemptorists began spending unbelievable amounts of time and energy filing official complaints about his personal defects. One confrere complained to local and Roman superiors that Father Seelos lacked experience, insight, and firmness as a superior and—the ultimate jab—he could not speak Latin well. Others complained that he was "an old mother" and "a blockhead." He was accused of being a pushover and criticized for allowing the students to play music after night prayers, to go swimming, and to put on school plays.

These may not seem like grave matters to us today, but in those days religious formation was highly structured and controlled. His program did not fit the rigid European model of religious formation, which was all that his superiors knew. He did not exactly break the rules, but he willingly bent them to accommodate the needs and culture of this first generation of American students. In short, he was a pioneer in his own Congregation, and some of his confreres were not ready for his progressive ideas.

The barrage of complaints and accusations resulted in his suddenly being declared "unfit" to direct the sixty students in religious formation. It was a humiliating dismissal, one that called into question Father Seelos's competence and example in religious life. Worse still, Father Nicholas Mauron, the superior general in Rome, made the decision without so much as informing Father Seelos of the accusations against him: Father Seelos had no opportunity to address them or to defend himself. It was terribly unfair.

Although he must have been shaken by the announcement, Father Seelos did not strike out in bitterness. His long, chatty letter of response to Father Mauron is cause enough for canonization. With cheerful courtesy, he thanks the superior general for his goodness and kindness to the Annapolis community and informs him that Father Gerard Dielemans, the new prefect imported from Europe, has arrived and settled in nicely. "The whole change went forward without any difficulty, because all were happy to see it as the greatest of blessings and accepted the new prefect with gratitude....I will be happy to go hand in hand with the new prefect and to help him wherever he may wish my help. It seems to me that the choice could not have fallen upon a better and more capable father, and I hope with full assurance that our loving God will certainly give his full blessing to this favor, given by your fatherly hand."

One thing is certain: Father Seelos did not regret giving up some of the responsibilities and burdens of leadership. Years before, he had written to his sister that he longed to relinquish his administrative duties—"Martha's work"—so that he could join Mary, "adoringly sitting at the feet of Jesus." Just two years earlier, Father Seelos had panicked upon hearing that he topped the list of candidates recommended by Michael O'Connor to succeed him as bishop of Pittsburgh. He wrote frantic letters to family and friends asking them to pray that his name be rejected. He went so far as to personally write an unflattering description of himself to Pope Pius IX. In fact, he was not chosen for this office—most likely because of his nationality more than any perceived deficits. Father Seelos celebrated his freedom that day by jubilantly granting all the students a "sparkling day of recreation."

7

MISSION PREACHER, PARISH PRIEST ONCE AGAIN, DEATH IN NEW ORLEANS

Shortly after his replacement arrived at the seminary, Father Seelos was appointed superior of the Redemptorist mission band. He continued to serve as superior of the Redemptorist community and pastor of St. Mary's parish, but for the next three years he was on the road. The members of the mission band traveled from parish to parish offering a careful program of sermons and spiritual exercises. Basic catechetical instruction and spiritual encouragement were sorely needed to bolster the faith of new immigrants in these initial years of American Catholic life.

Usually, at least two Redemptorists gave the mission; in larger parishes, up to six Redemptorists participated. The purpose of the missions was threefold: to strengthen and renew the spiritual life of the active members of a parish, to invite lapsed Catholics back to the practice of the faith, and to win converts. A typical Redemptorist mission lasted from one to two weeks, with sermons and conferences presented on consecutive nights and confessions offered day and night. Confession was considered the high point of the mission; the missionaries spent up to twelve hours a day in the confessional. Then as now, the Redemptorist mission as instituted by Saint Alphonsus Liguori was a brilliant evangelization tool that yielded a rich and continual harvest of new and renewed Christians.

Between 1862 and 1865, the Redemptorists averaged over twenty-three missions each year, crisscrossing the Midwest and the eastern United States. Despite the difficulties of travel during wartime—slow, cramped trains, "jammed with unkempt soldiers, all indulging in ribald jokes and coarse language"—the Redemptorists were galvanized by the success of the missions and touched by the dedication and devotion of so many Catholics, starved for spiritual renewal, who traveled up to thirty miles to hear the missionaries.

Father Seelos preached missions in Missouri, Illinois, Wisconsin, Michigan, Ohio, Pennsylvania, New York, New Jersey, Connecticut, and Rhode Island. "I love the work of the missions more than anything else," he gushed in a letter to his sister in 1863. "It is properly *the* work in the vineyard of the Lord; it is entirely apostolic work."

The people were habitually moved to tears by the missionaries' impassioned pleas to dedicate their lives anew to Jesus Christ, the Redeemer. "In Him is Plentiful Redemption!" was and still is the exuberant Redemptorist motto.

Everywhere the missionaries went, they preached the good news of God's inexhaustible love for his people. Father Seelos wrote, "The assistance of power from above is plainly visible, so that we are often humbled at seeing the great mercy and goodness of God." At the end of one mission, according to Father Seelos, the people were so carried away by feelings of gratitude that they almost picked up the Redemptorists and carried them off in their arms!

Many caught what someone described as "Seelos fever"; during the missions, "everybody flocked to him for confession, instruction, and consolation." One of the reasons he was so successful in the confessional is that he never rushed his penitents, no matter how many were waiting. He sincerely wanted to hear as much of the penitent's life story as possible to try to understand the reason behind any fault or sin. His personal motto was *Non multa, sed multum* (Not many, but much).

One confrere asked Father Seelos after he had stayed in the confessional an hour longer than the others how many additional confessions he had heard. "One," Father Seelos answered simply. "What!" the confrere blurted, aghast. "Only one?" He replied, *"Unum, sed leonem,"* (One, but it was a lion). Not surprisingly, at the end of a mission Father Seelos was often completely exhausted from hearing confessions.

In a moment of weariness, no doubt, Father Seelos gave vent to one persistent frustration. "I don't have any special sufferings, although the life of a religious cannot be without its crosses, nor should it be," he wrote to his sister. "Love of my holy vocation makes everything easy for me. But I'm sorry about one thing: that in this I am again to function as superior. When will I finally be a subordinate subject again, when, be able to simply obey!"

In 1865, Father Seelos's desire to live as simple subject was fulfilled. Between November 1865 and September 1866 he was assigned to Saint Mary's in Detroit, Michigan, where he assisted in parish ministry. Although his stay was brief, he made a lasting impression on Bishop Peter Paul Lefevere of Detroit who remarked, "I am sorry that Father Seelos must leave my diocese, for one has only to look at him to know that he is a saint."

Father Francis Van Emstede, the superior of the Detroit Redemptorist community, was similarly impressed when he followed up on the list of sick calls that Father Seelos had entrusted to him upon his departure. A confrere recalled, "When [Father Van Emstede] saw the poverty and wretchedness of these people and they told him how Father Seelos had been their friend and consoler, he well realized why they liked him."

St. Mary's church, New Orleans

The confreres who knew him best said that Father Seelos enjoyed visiting the sick almost as much as he enjoyed preaching missions, dedicating entire days to this ministry when he was able. Since he himself had known sickness off and on since childhood, he was able to understand the suffering and loneliness of the ill and knew how to comfort them. He would never just say the customary prayers and hurry off; he would pull up a chair to chat awhile, read aloud from the sick person's favorite book, or otherwise keep him or her company.

On September 27, 1866, Father Seelos was transferred to St. Mary's Assumption parish in New Orleans. It was a difficult and dangerous city: dangerous because the warm, wet climate harbored disease; difficult because immigrants of various nationalities were swarming into the area, brawling and competing for jobs. At this time, New Orleans was second only to New York as a point of entry for immigrants into the U.S.

Father John Duffy

Father Seelos was ecstatic upon receiving news of his appointment. Most of the members of the Redemptorist community in New Orleans had been his students at one time or another; they received their beloved mentor with joy. Father John Duffy, the superior of the New Orleans community, went so far as to claim that he loved Father Seelos more than his own mother.

The reminiscences of another former student, Father Benedict Neithart, provide a charming snapshot of Father Seelos's blissful final year of life.

All of the fathers and brothers here who had known Father Seelos as rector and prefect of students at the North often remarked that he seemed much happier than he had ever been before. He never looked careworn; no responsibilities bore him down; no anxieties clouded his noble brow. His walk was light and elastic; his laughter hearty and ringing; his features as calm as the cloudless sky; his heart a perpetual feast. At times he could not repress his interior joy, and he would then exclaim, with his hand on his heart: "*Hier ist's gut sein, im lichten warmen Suden; als gemeiner Soldat.*" ("It's good to be here, in the sunny and warm south, as an ordinary soldier!") I have now made the round of all the houses. Here is my home; here I'll live with a book in a nook. Here I'll rest my bones in the grave; for I think I have wandered enough.

By this time Father Seelos was widely regarded as a holy man. People continued to be attracted to him, to confide in him, and to call for him when they were sick. Some reported that remarkable conversions and cures followed his visits. Others said simply that they felt more lighthearted or hopeful after spending time in his presence. But in God's plan Father Seelos's time of ministry in New Orleans would be short.

In the fall of 1867, an especially virulent outbreak of yellow fever paralyzed New Orleans. One third of the city's one hundred fifty thousand residents contracted the virus; five thousand died. On September 17, Father Seelos fell victim himself. Characteristically, his last pastoral act was to visit another man dying of the disease. Although he was feeling poorly that day, he walked a considerable distance to care for the man and stayed with him until the end. He returned home at three in the afternoon and collapsed into his bed.

At first, Father Seelos's confreres thought that he had a mild case of the fever. But then one of his lungs collapsed, and he lost his appetite. His infirmarian, Brother Louis Kenning, asked him whether there was anything that still needed to be done in regard to legacies and such. His sense of humor intact, Father Seelos replied, "No, nothing at all. Before I came to America, we took care of everything....I get nothing and they also get nothing."

When he became delirious, his confreres knew that the end was near. Nevertheless, there were moments of levity as his Redemptorist brothers kept watch. One night, in a temporary delirium, Father Seelos gesticulated wildly and preached in French, English, and German on a certain Scripture text.

Afterward he fell asleep. Soon he awoke again with a start and said, "Where am I? Am I dead?" The confreres in the room burst out laughing.

At daybreak on Friday, October 4, he seemed visibly weaker than the previous day. The confreres gathered around his bed, some kneeling, one holding a candle, and they began to recite the prayers for the dying. Suddenly, someone got the idea that they could ease the death of Father Seelos more by singing than by prayer. When they asked Father Seelos if he would like this, he smiled and nodded. Together, they sang one of Father Seelos's favorite Marian hymns, "Gentle Queen." Brother Louis later wrote,

> It will strike everyone as strange how we could still sing at such a time, but I have to admit that the sick man visibly obtained relief from it; he seemed entirely animated by it and freed from his sufferings, looking up as if he already saw the heavens opening. When we noticed this, we also obtained relief....and so in this way, Father Seelos slumbered gently and quietly, without convulsions or straining, over into a better life.

Father Seelos died at age forty-eight, just before six in the evening, on October 4, 1867, a Friday. Immediately after death he was robed in priestly vestments, laid in a coffin, and waked at Saint Mary's Assumption church.

That night, even though a storm raged, as soon as the church bell tolled the sad message that Father Seelos was dead, his friends and admirers began to trickle into the church.

In the morning, the trickle became a stream, and then a flood. During the three weeks of his illness, the daily newspapers in New Orleans had published regular updates on his condition. His death was front-page news on the morning of October 5. Rich, poor, black, white, new immigrants and native-born citizens, came from all parts of the city to see him one last time and to pay their respects. They brought rosaries, medals, and prayer books to touch to the casket or to the hands of the body. "Yes, the crowd was so great," Brother Louis reported, "that I and a server placed ourselves near the body so that the candles and everything else wouldn't be knocked over."

After the solemn *Requiem*, the coffin was carried

by four lay brothers and laymen in procession around Saint Mary's Assumption church and then lowered into the crypt. Today his remains rest in a sacred reliquary where many come to pray and pay tribute.

Just before his assignment to New Orleans, Father Seelos had said, "Now I have been in all the houses that we have in America, except not yet in New Orleans. But if I get there, I will stay there to die there." The boy who wanted to follow the footsteps of Saint Francis Xavier had reached his heavenly home.

EPILOGUE

Father Seelos died on October 4, 1867, in New Orleans on a stormy Friday evening and was buried the following day in Saint Mary Assumption Church amid the great sorrow of the parishioners who packed the church to overflowing. But when his mortal remains were lowered into a crypt in the floor of the sanctuary, his memory was not buried with him. There was too much to remember about him and too many who did not want, or could not, forget this very holy and kindly man.

There were, of course, those whose lives had been radically touched by his preaching, by his teaching, by his gentle but firm counsel in the confessional. There were those whose most precious souvenir of him were the letters of consolation and spiritual advice that he had written them and which they could not get themselves to destroy. We have seen in the biography the many ways that Father Seelos made God real and lovable to those who came under the influence of his own loving life and priestly work. We must not, however, forget or pass over some other ways in which Father Seelos made the unseen world visible to others and brought God's kindness and power to bear in their lives.

In Pittsburgh, even as a very young priest, Father Seelos gained the reputation of obtaining extraordinary favors from God. There was little Philomena, whose epileptic seizures were so terrible and for whom doctors could do nothing, that her mother asked Father Seelos to pray that God take her to himself. Instead, Father Seelos prayed over her and she was cured. A cripple, so the account goes, came one day to the rectory and asked to speak with Father Seelos. As soon as they were in the parlor, the cripple hobbled to the open window, threw his crutches out into the garden, and said that he would not leave until Father Seelos gave him a blessing and cured him. Father Seelos did bless him and the man walked out unaided. And there were similar wonderful favors received through his prayers wherever Father Seelos ministered.

As was noted, Father Seelos had a widespread renown as a wise and kindly confessor. But for many, there was more to going to confession to Father Seelos. An attorney in Pittsburgh remarked that when he knelt before him "a singular power pervaded me." A Carmelite nun noted that he "knew my inner life before I told him about it." A New Orleans woman said that in going to confession to him you knew that you were in the presence of a saint. A carpenter in Baltimore observed that Father Seelos in the confessional exercised a certain power over those with whom no one else could do anything.

And then, too, there were unusual ways in which Father Seelos gave others an experience of the mysterious hidden world of God. In Cumberland, Maryland, a Redemptorist brother went into the quiet chapel one afternoon and there saw Father Seelos with his arms stretched out in the form of a cross "suspended about a foot off the ground." A Redemptorist father was convinced that Father Seelos could see into the future because he had predicted something about his brother that at the time was very improbable but actually did come to pass. On the train going to New Orleans in 1866, when a nun asked him how long he was going to stay in New Orleans, he answered calmly, "For one year and then I'll die of yellow fever," which is exactly what happened.

A young carriage driver in New Orleans, bedridden with yellow fever, called for Father Seelos. When he entered the room, as the man stated, "I saw him surrounded by a brilliant light"; and he insisted that he had full use of his senses and that there was no other light in the room. A middle-aged widow, recalling her school days, testified that when he came to the school "the classroom seemed illuminated with a certain supernatural brilliance," and Father Seelos "seemed surrounded by rays of heavenly light." A twenty-year-old baker in New Orleans reported that he noticed Father Seelos one day on the street but could hardly recognize him. There "was something angelic about his appearance" that impressed him and filled him with an overpowering experience of joy.

These unusual signs of God's presence in the life of Father Seelos and the witness of the love of God and neighbor manifested in his every action were not missed by others. Brother Louis Kenning, who nursed him during his final sickness, wrote in his journal that "everyone who has ever known him considers him a saint and rightly so, for he is one." On the second anniversary of the death of Father Seelos, Brother wrote to the Redemptorist superior general in Rome, urging him to encourage the American provincial superior "to take care that some things be written up and preserved" about Father Seelos by those who knew him more closely, less they be lost forever.

The words of Brother Louis did not go unheeded. For little over a decade, letters and manuscripts of Father Seelos were collected and those who knew him or lived with him were asked to write up their remembrances. By 1883, enough material was on hand to enable Father John Berger, C.Ss.R., nephew and first biographer of Saint John Neumann and a student under Father Seelos, to begin a biography. Hardly had he set his hand to this work when he died unexpectedly. The biography was completed by Peter Zimmer, C.Ss.R., another student of Father Seelos, and was published in 1887, *Leben und Wirken des Hochwürdigen P. Franz Seelos, aus der Congregation des allerheiligsten Erlösers.*

The tomb of Father Seelos in New Orleans became a place of pilgrimage for those who sought his intercession in all their needs. Favors received were many. The ordinary people were convinced of his holiness and the power of his prayers; it was time now to seek the official recognition of the Church. Between 1900 and 1903, four ecclesiastical investigations were conducted: in Pittsburgh, Baltimore, New Orleans, and Augsburg, Germany. In them, sixty-seven witnesses were interrogated about the virtuous life and work of Father Seelos; of these, fifty-seven were eyewitnesses who had known him personally. Transcripts of the testimony were sent to Rome with the hope that, within a short time, the process of canonization of Father Seelos would be accepted by the Vatican and move along smoothly and successfully. But things were to be otherwise; in fact much otherwise.

For reasons that are not clear even to expert students of the canonization process of Father Seelos, matters rested until 1970 when the Congregation for the Causes of Saints officially accepted Father Francis Xavier Seelos as a candidate for sainthood, and gave him the title "Servant of God."

In the meantime, however, his reputation for holiness among the people did not die out. His devotees remembered him through the long years and continued to come to his burial place in Saint Mary Assumption, New Orleans, to ask for his help; and their prayers were heard. In the early 1960s, the Seelos Center was established near his tomb to handle the increasing number of requests for information about him, and a monthly newsletter, *Father Seelos and Sanctity,* began to appear. The average number of letters received each month in 1999 was over seventeen hundred. To make the general public more familiar with Father Seelos, a thoroughly researched biography by Michael J. Curley, C.Ss.R., was published in 1969, *Cheerful Ascetic: The Life of Francis Xavier Seelos, C.Ss.R.*

On the official ecclesiastical level, progress was

being made throughout the intervening years. Study and research continued on writing a biography of the life and sanctity of Father Seelos that was based both on the testimony of the witnesses of the four 1900–1903 investigations, as well as on documentary evidence. This project was entrusted to Carl Hoegerl, C.Ss.R., who completed his work in 1998, *Documentary Study of the Life, Virtues, and Fame for Holiness of the Servant of God, Francis Xavier Seelos, Professed Priest of the Congregation of the Most Holy Redeemer.* This documented biography was approved by six historians on December 14, 1999, and by eight theologians on January 5, 2000. In the presence of His Holiness, Pope John Paul II, a decree was promulgated on January 27, 2000, declaring that Father Seelos had practiced the Christian virtues in an heroic degree. He thereby obtained the title, "Venerable Father Seelos."

On the same day, January 27, also in the presence of His Holiness, Pope John Paul II, a decree was promulgated attributing a miraculous cure to the intercession of Father Seelos. In 1966, Mrs. Angela Boudreaux was diagnosed with a massive and inoperable malignancy that had nearly destroyed her liver. The attending physician was convinced that she did not have a chance of survival. The trust, however, that she put in the help of Father Seelos prevailed, because in two or three weeks she was back to normal. The doctor recalls this as the most remarkable case of his many years in the medical profession. The way was now clear for the solemn ceremony of beatification in Saint Peter's Square, April 9, 2000. Father Seelos now has the title, "Blessed Francis Seelos."

Blessed Francis did not make a great impression on the world at large; nor even was he remarkable, as ecclesiastical historians consider it, in the history of the Church at large. However, on the ordinary level of Catholic life he did much and he has much to offer and to say to the modern world, even though he died so long ago in the middle of the nineteenth century. Simply put, his message goes like this: If you want to be happy, try to be holy; if you want to be very happy, try to be very holy. It's as simple as that. His very happy life was a perfect example of that: he was always happy, always cheerful, even in the midst of difficult and trying times, because he always tried to keep close to God and to the Blessed Mother; he always tried to be very holy.

The Church tells us that Blessed Francis practiced the Christian virtues in an heroic degree, but where are the heroics? There aren't any. That's the message of his life. Father Seelos tells us that you do not have to do the things that the world in general, or showtime, says are great and heroic. All you have to do is live your life, as God has ordained it for you, in the best way you know how and every day. Everyone can do that: married or single; homemaker, office worker, carpenter, salesman—everyone. The heroics consist in doing it all the time and to please God. That's the way Father Seelos did it. He was just a simple priest who every day of his life tried to be holy, tried to do God's will wherever that might lead him, tried to do what he could for others, especially the most needy. He tried to be like Jesus all the time. And because he did this, he was happy, very happy, always happy. That's his word to you: Be holy, be happy!

Prayer to
BLESSED FRANCIS
XAVIER SEELOS

O Lord,
my strength and my Redeemer,
let the words of my mouth
and the meditation of my heart
be pleasing in Your sight.
I offer praise to You
for the grace You have bestowed
on Your humble missionary,
Blessed Francis Xavier Seelos.
May I have the same joyful vigor
that Father Seelos possessed
during his earthly life
to love You deeply
and live faithfully Your gospel.
Amen.

Divine Physician,
You infused Blessed Francis Xavier Seelos
with the gift of Your healing.
By the help of his prayers,
sustain in me the grace to know Your will
and the strength to overcome my afflictions.
For love of You, make me whole.
May I learn from the example of Blessed Seelos
and gain comfort from his patient endurance.
Amen.

Bountiful God,
in Blessed Francis Xavier Seelos
You have given Your people
a model for those who labor joyfully
in Your earthly kingdom.
May the smile of Father Seelos
in Your heavenly dominion
dwell on those who find life burdensome.
Keep continually before our eyes
the gentleness of Jesus Christ, our Redeemer.
Amen.

BYRON MILLER, C.Ss.R.

APPENDICES

Excerpts From the Letters
of Blessed Francis Xavier Seelos, C.Ss.R.

This letter, written to a family at Saint Alphonsus parish in Baltimore on July 18, 1857, shows Father Seelos's practical understanding of the responsibilities of parents.

> If...the conscientious rearing of children is accompanied with great blessing from God even in this life, in the next it will be rewarded with indescribable joy. Or, is there no joy in the thought that all your children will thank you for all eternity that with so much effort, so many cares and fears, you were concerned day and night about their eternal salvation.

In the following letter, Father Seelos reveals some of his guiding principles in his method of spiritual direction. The recipient of this letter was seeking advice on dealing with her interior trials. Father Seelos wrote this letter on January 1, 1858.

> I am encouraged by the infinite goodness of God whose punishment and chastisement are nothing but signs of his love. Saint Paul says: "The child he accepts he chastises" (Heb 12:6). I am encouraged by that love of God with which he leads us along the rough road upon which he first led his most beloved and First-born Son. Yes, I am encouraged by the thought that the poorest, most sorrowful, most despised, rejected, martyred, crucified, and dying Son of God is our only and greatest model by which we are to judge ourselves.

> [D]earest Lady, what is the staff that I give you for your journey on the narrow and steep way that leads to the narrow door through which we enter into the house of life and peace? The staff is no other than the holy cross that we must carry each day. It carries us each day until at last it serves as a bridge that leads us across the abyss of death into life eternal. If each day, dear Lady,

you are convinced and believe that you have to carry a cross in order to be a faithful servant of Jesus, it is, indeed, certain that this thought will give you great courage, because you will then see it as an honor to be counted among the faithful servants of the crucified Redeemer....

When we seem abandoned by God and are rejected by others, where can we find peace, where are we to lay down our head? Our only consolation comes from looking at our model Jesus, who is without consolation, and to the suffering Mother of sorrows. Only these are to be our comfort.

Therefore, good Lady, boast of your weakness, because our loving God protects his weakest children the most, and loves them the most and takes care of them the best of all. Admit your weakness, take your flight to prayer, go hand in hand with God, and all will go well.

Father Seelos is writing to his two sisters Damiana and Romualda Seelos who have also followed him in a religious vocation. This letter, written on August 10, 1858, is a newsy yet deeply spiritual letter of a young priest to his family, telling of such various matters as bugs and ticks, well-meaning parishioners who would prepare an overabundance of meals for the ailing Father Seelos, the crush of pastoral work and its incessant demands, the beauties of celebrating Forty Hours' Devotion, and the sad state of the practice of Catholicism in the United States. In the following excerpt, Father Seelos shows his humble nature:

> But my dearest Sisters, you know that I, a second Prodigal Son, have squandered the whole big inheritance of divine grace, and my virtuous life is like a rumpled and much patched garment. And I never feel my wretchedness more than when in addition to this I have vain and proud thoughts. ...For this reason I cannot really become proud. ...If my higher superiors were to ask it, I would gladly become a lay brother and would be extremely happy. But, unfortunately, I am of less use there, because I do not understand anything about practical matters.

> If someone from those around us were actually to treat us with violence, we could still draw from it even the greatest of benefits, because it would be a kind of innocent suffering, a genuine imitation of the innocent crucified Jesus. Nothing would

be sweeter in its fruits; nothing would be more comforting in our misery....We have really committed so many thousands of mistakes for which we have not yet been punished, and for which, perhaps, a terrible Purgatory awaits us. How gladly should we not now and again be willing to suffer something innocently.

For all the saints this [obedience] was the beginning of their virtue and their penance and their humility. In this consisted their constant effort toward progress and this was its perfection. They were merely faithful in little things. If sometimes they were not, they cried over it...and made up in humility what was lacking in fidelity.

In the next letter, written by Father Seelos to his mother and family between September 24 and October 2, 1859, he relates in detail, some of his pastoral experiences with the people of Cumberland, where he was not only prefect of students and professor but also pastor of the parish of Saints Peter and Paul. In one very personal paragraph, he thanks his mother for encouraging him in devotion of Our Lady.

Dear Mother, how I want to thank you for instilling into us children a great devotion to Mary; such a legacy from parents is worth more than gold or silver. I hope that all my brothers and sisters have a really great devotion to Mary. Our departed father especially gave us all such a beautiful example in this regard, even on his death bed, and could not stop placing all his trust in Mary and Joseph, who, next to the Divine Redeemer, must be our chief patrons.

APPENDIX B

Excerpts From the Mission Chronicles Reporting the Work of Blessed Francis Xavier Seelos, C.Ss.R.

The following excerpts are from a record that tells of the conditions and consequences of the missions and retreats given by Father Seelos between the years 1863, when he became superior of the mission band, and 1866, when he was no longer superior but still conducted some parish missions. From this record, it can be seen that Father Seelos traveled far and wide, in many difficult situations, under laborious travel conditions, and with poor accommodations. Among the places he ministered were Chicago (Illinois), Toledo, Cincinnati, and Cleveland (Ohio), Providence (Rhode Island), Buffalo, and New York (New York), and even as far West as St. Louis (Missouri). These excerpts are taken from the *Chronicle of the Missions Given by Redemptorist Fathers in the United States of N. America* and give evidence that the itinerant Redemptorist preachers, serving the first immigrants to the United States from Europe, were giants of the faith.

This mission [in Waukegan, Illinois, October 4–17, 1863] was a very difficult one....What we had to contend against most was enmity. There were in Waukegan persons who had kept up the most bitter enmities for years and years, and what was worse than all else, not only women, but men even lived in enmity. To give an idea of these enmities, there was a woman who was obliged by one of the Fathers to go see a man and to speak to him. She was willing and went four miles to see the man, who was in bed in a dying condition. She went on her knees and implored him in his dying moments to pardon her. He turned his back on her and the woman had to leave the house unreconciled.

The congregation of Woodstock [Illinois] is a very small one....The church was however well filled during the mission [given on October 18–24, 1863]. What we had to battle most against was the terrible vice of drunkenness and also the grog-shops. We succeeded in checking these evils, whether with permanent success or not the renewal will best tell.

This was indeed a hard mission [given in Hartland, Illinois, October 25–November 7, 1863]. The church was over a mile distant from the priest's house....The weather was also very unfavorable and it was a scene to behold the missionaries packed on a lumber wagon, wending their way to the church and home again, dripping with rain and shivering with cold.

During the mission [given in Chicago on December 13–15, 1863] the men as well as the women manifested great zeal and though the weather was sometimes cold yet the church was always filled. Some evenings it was literally packed, so that it seemed to be one immense sea of human heads. This was the case especially at the dedication to the Blessed Virgin Mary and at the erection of the cross. At the latter ceremony, the people were so moved that...all wept and sobbed aloud.

APPENDIX C

Excerpts From the Sermons
of Blessed Francis Xavier Seelos, C.Ss.R.

The following excerpts are from two mission sermons—one on the mercy of God and one on prayer—which were delivered by Father Seelos. Given his genial nature and his affinity for prayer, Father Seelos probably found both these topics close to his heart—the heart of a mission preacher who followed in the path of Saint Alphonsus.

Yes, my beloved people, God is merciful and his mercy is, as the prophet says, above all his works and, as the Blessed Virgin sings in her beautiful song of praise, his mercy is from generation to generation to all that fear him....If you therefore wish to live hereafter in the service and fear of God; if you sincerely repent and amend your life; if you forsake forever all those evil ways in order to follow Christ in self-denial and penance; if you really prepare for the life to come, rejoice, for here I present you the balm for all your wounds—the infinite mercy of God.

O sinner, behold the mercy of God. After having offended him, after having forsaken him, after having preferred sinning to him, he has not yet abandoned you entirely for he speaks to you, calls upon you, invites you to penance, offers you his mercy: "Behold, I stand at the door and knock!"

Men, says Saint Chrysostom, are slow in building up and quick in tearing down, and the saint is right, even in America, where the largest and finest buildings are quickly built up; for to tear them down, if required, is the work of a moment. But quite different it is with God: he was very quick in building up the whole universe and it required but a word and worlds were created. ... But the same quickness of building up we find with God in his work of grace. Saint David, Saint Paul, Saint Magdalen, the Good Thief on the Cross—a moment was necessary to make them saints and raise them from the lowest state of sin and passion to a very high degree of perfection and sanctity.

God's most earnest desire is to give us his grace, since he wishes the salvation of all; but he gives it under certain conditions. And by neglecting these conditions, he also neglects the means of salvation of all; but he gives it under certain conditions. And by neglecting these conditions, he also neglects the means of salvation. Now, what are the conditions under which God gives grace and strength. I can answer by one word: "*Prayer.*"

[A]s Christians, we are obliged to pray in the name of Jesus: "Whatsoever you ask the Father in my name, he will give it to you" (Jn 14:13). But what do we mean when we say that we are obliged to pray in the name of Jesus. It means to pray as our Savior would pray, if placed in our condition.

Our Savior was accustomed to pray in solitude, in the desert, on the mountain, retired from the people, during the night, when all around was silent. And even in the Old Testament, the people are blamed for not praying earnestly. "With their lips they glorify me but their heart is far from me" (Isa 29:13).

[I]s it possible for us to pray always, to be continually in church, or say the rosary and other prayers the livelong day?...In order to be well understood, I will here make a comparison. As food is the nourishment of the body, so prayer is the nourishment of the soul. We eat daily in order to preserve life and we are obliged to pray daily in order to preserve the life of our soul, which is the grace of God. But you eat not only once a day but several times, and if you are particularly fatigued and weak you take some extraordinary refreshments. The very same is to be observed with regard to prayer. Your soul requires refreshment several times a day, and if you are severely tempted, and if you feel the weakness of the flesh, you stand more in need of God's grace.